i hope this reaches her too

There will be men who never show up but will claim to miss you. There will be men who claim to love you while treating you like shit. There will be men who tell lies and yet expect you to believe them. There will be men who betray you and yet they'll still expect you to trust them. There will be men who say all the right things but their actions will never match what they speak. There will be men who claim to be sorry then continue to do the things they're always apologizing for. There will be men who won't claim you but expect you to bear their child. There will be men who will fall short in every area they need them to excel in. There will be men who will make you hate the fact that you care about them. These men were never worth it. These men are never worth it. These men don't deserve your energy. These men no longer deserve your attention. Stay away from these types of men. Walk away from this type of man. There will be men who are nothing but lessons and examples of what to avoid as you move forward with your life and you once you move forward with your life, avoid these types of men as much as you can. There is love, an honest love. A deep love, the type of love that provides peace. There is a love that will outlast the pain and overshadow all of the aches in your heart but in order to find it, you have to practice letting go of those who are content with letting you down. These men, the men described in this passage will serve as stepping stones to someone who is better than all of them.

I know you're hurting because of someone from your past. Someone who is able to remain current while currently hurting you. I see your smile for what it truly is, a visual representation of how powerful your heart has been. I have these moments where I wish I could peel back the layers of your soul and kiss the parts of you that'll relieve the pain. I'd even go as far to retrieve that pain and make it my own, an effort to show you that you're not alone but you don't even need that. You don't even need me. You don't even need another soul to take whole of you because all you've ever had is yourself and that has always been more than enough.

I know you're hurting because of someone from your past and I won't try to save you but I'll just sit here, I'll wait for as long as you need me to. I'll be here waiting for you on the other side of victory.

She has pain in her eyes, I fool myself into thinking that I can see the stains on her cheek from the tears that she's cried but there's love in her heart. I think it's the way she's taken interest in what I have to say that causes me to become more interested in everything she's been through. The way she wraps her mind around my thoughts is what makes me want to tell her more. I open her up by being more open with my own truths. My words like fingertips on her skin almost as if she's applying lotion and I, the emotional moisture. We touch without touching, we connect in a deeper sense. We've hidden ourselves for so long and it feels good to finally see one another.

I sit and wonder if she knows that I'll be hers before the year is up or that within the time it takes to write this, I've already captured the inner most parts of her mind in which I crave the most. Impossible to find the right terms as I write terms that pale & fail in comparison to her but I'll do my best. Come be my Sun, be the warmth in my heart or my moon, the gentle light in the darkness that attempts to plague my life. Live in peace where I reside, be my daytime as well as my night. I wonder if she knows.. I wrote this with my soul. I wonder if she realizes that I wrote this for her.

You are a woman and what this means is that you have this transformative power to take rage and create peace. You are a woman and what this means is that you have the ability to take pain and create a version of power that helps you conquer whatever or whomever attempts to tear you down.

You are a woman and this makes you mighty. Never forget this..

let them leave
if they want to
you're truly rare
so much that not everyone
knows how to love you
and that's okay

because happiness and peace
is only achieved
when you let go of those
who hurt your soul

without the compliments
there's still a beauty
that lives within you

without a relationship
you are still valuable
even while alone
you are love, you are loved

stop searching for what you deserve
outside of yourself
you are already everything
you're supposed to be
and you already have
everything you'll ever need

there will come a moment
where you finally wake up
not specifically physically
but emotionally

you realize that those who hurt you
were never actually worth
your tears
and the ones you fought for
were never truly deserving
of an emotional response

this realization is sad
but beautiful all at once
an emotional enlightenment

she knew what she wanted
she knew what she needed
she knew what she deserved

determined not to settle
she chose to be single
even if it meant time alone

instead of wasting her love
she would rather just stand alone
because being with herself
meant having everything she needed

even though she loves you
even though she cares
even though moving on
will be one of the most difficult
things she'll ever have to do
even though she'd rather not
live a life that doesn't include you

she'll do it
she'll manage
she'll get there

to the eyes reading this page
reading these words
i hope you build up the courage
to leave behind anyone
who restricts you from being happy

you have a love
that not just anyone
can understand

you have a heart
too large for most hands

and this is why you're single
and better off on your own
until you find someone
worthy of caring for

all in a sudden
you're the one
texting first
and even then
those conversations
are cut short by one-word replies
and or delayed responses

things are different now

while they're letting go of you
you're still trying to hold on
and that's what hurts you in the end

Maybe you don't always let go
because you stopped caring. I think you get
to a point of realizing that you can only
control what you do in your relationship and
if they're not willing to change then they're
no longer worthy of your effort.

This year might have been one of the hardest years you've experienced. There were many changes in which have put you in a place of emotional concern. All in all, you've remained strong in areas where others may have expected you to fail but you always find a way to survive. You'll always continue to press forward.

This is the confirmation you've been searching for. This is the message you need. It's time to walk away, it's okay to want more for yourself. It's okay to leave behind the person who refuses to help you cultivate a healthy relationship.

If he doesn't speak to your soul then there's no point in entertaining anything he has to say.

If she doesn't speak to your soul then there's no point in entertaining anything she has to say.

If they're not speaking to your soul then there's no point in entertaining anything they have to say.

You're a Queen, struggling with the fact that it's time to let go but you're strong enough to walk away, providing yourself with an opportunity to be found by someone who will love you as you deserve. I know it's difficult but I believe in you and your ability to do what is needed. I know it's easier said than done but you were created with the strength to survive anything. You got this.

THIS IS THE CYCLE THAT NEEDS TO END, NOW.

Every time he fucks up and realizes that you're ready to walk away, he does something nice to make you stay. You give him chance after chance, hoping for a bit of change but it never happens, things remain the same and this is a deadly cycle that needs to end, now.

You're a diamond in a world that prefers rhinestones and that's okay. You're not meant for everyone and most of them don't deserve you.

She keeps her guard up because most guys
just want to fuck and waste her time.

The problem is, you gave your heart to someone who just wanted a nut and used love as a means to get what he wanted. This is who they are, this is what the weak ones do. Promise you things they were never willing to provide.

Authentic love only.

Your ex will waste your time, stress you out
and neglect you then expect you to take
them seriously as " just a friend.. "

WAKE UP.
YOU DESERVE BETTER.

SOMEONE NEW.

1:11

unbothered by the storms
she became lighting
she became rain

she went cold
then ignited
her own flame

i am the author and poet
of your emotions
helping you discover
the truths you struggle
to find

i hope you find someone
with a crazy that matches yours

no clubs
no parties
rather lay up
under you

i'm sorry
but you're not a princess
and witches definitely don't exist
this will never be a fairytale
or some enchanting story
of science fiction

you live in the real world
your pain is a real thing
and life can be tough
but aren't you tougher
than this life

perfection is nonexistent
but this doesn't mean
you don't deserve a portion
of happiness and joy

perfection is nonexistent
but this doesn't mean
you don't deserve
to be loved

you're not a damsel in distress
at best
you are a fucking warrior
willing to fight your way
toward everything
you believe you deserve

KEEP FIGHTING!

Attraction is common, it's too easy. I want
something deeper, a soul connection, a
lifetime partner, a soul mate. I'm tired of
starting over, I want a love that feels infinite.
I want a love that never stops.

Essentially, true love is talking to someone who is capable of making you forget that you're not okay and I hope you find that.

i know you feel invisible
but someone will see you
the right one will see

until then
you need to see yourself

sweet soul
you have always been the moon
and sadly, he could never
appreciate your night sky

Giving love only to feel rejected is the worst feeling. You begin to feel as if you're not good enough and the love you have within yourself is insufficient. That type of rejection causes you to pull away from the person who only seems to be doing more of what pushes you away. You finally get enough courage to fall in love but it's not what you expect because you're in love with the wrong person. The right one will never make you feel like the love you've shared isn't enough. Instead, the one who truly cares for your soul will mirror the love you've share with them.

So damaged emotionally that when someone comes along ready and willing to provide what you deserve, you don't know how to respond.

Patience is key. Yours as well as the person who is after your heart. If what they speak unto to you is true, they'll fight for you until you allow them to fight beside you.

My message to those who have been hurt loving the wrong person. Your love is still valuable, you are still good enough and you deserve the type of love that reflects your value. I know it's hard, it just takes time with someone who refuses to give up on you.

The night comes for you as if you owe it.
Midnight arrives to collect everything that
you've kept hidden and you just sit there
refusing to look it in the eye in hopes that
night sky will fade behind the sun.

BE STRONG.

I see you laying there in darkness, your emotions on life support because the thought of him is killing you. The pain comes in waves and in this moment you feel as if you're drowning. I can feel it, it's like I feel you. Smiling all damn day but fuck it, I see the real you. He was supposed to be your protector, words like knives, who knew he'd try to kill your joy and destroy your peace.

You're laying there reading this, closer to the edge you stand. Every night, you're closer and I know it, so I decided to speak to you in this moment. Listen, you're good enough and that has nothing to do with anyone but you. In this moment, I need you to understand that you were made special. You don't have to put up with someone who puts you down. He's given you nothing but pain and that's something you don't deserve. He's given you nothing, so in his absence you lose nothing. Understand that his absence gives you an opportunity to find peace, the peace that lives within yourself, the peace in which he's caused you to suppress. You might feel like this every night this year but remember every word written here. I know your heart has scars, I know you're tired and the only way to find rest is to let go. I believe in you!!

you mean something
don't give up
don't give in

you mean something
even when you feel like you don't

you mean something
even when you feel like breaking
you are strong
even during moments of weakness

don't give up
don't give in

You're not like anything they'd ever seen. I mean your existence is proof of angels walking the earth prepared to raise hell if you need to. So much of who you are is a lot that they'll never understand and only a chosen few will ever deserve to sit next to you. I know sometimes you don't feel like it, there are moments where you forget about the strength that resides within your heart. There are times when the heaviness of it all comes to weigh you down without warning. There are days and night that feel more like twisted nightmares of everything you struggle to get away from but you mustn't run. You mustn't run because you are capable of destroying everything that chases you.

Why do for a man who refuses to do anything for you..

Why try harder for a man who refuses to try for you…

He wants you to treat him like a boyfriend or husband mean while he's content with treating you like a secret, like something or someone he's ashamed of.

Fuck that, move on.

You have to stop choosing heartache over joy. You have to stop choosing sleepless nights over rest. You have to stop choosing the person who has chosen to fight you instead of for you.

she wanted to know what it felt like to be
with someone who would adore her deeply
and so, she fell for herself

she was ready to walk away from all the
things that no longer gave her peace

she believed that she deserved more and so
she walked away to find it

she was tired and so she stopped trying for
the person who stopped trying for her

she kept going
she kept fighting
she continued to survive
she refused to quit
she chose herself
she was all that she need

Somewhere between being hopeful and having your heart broken, you lost your smile and your ability to be happy and I hope you learn to piece yourself back together because you deserve to know what it means to find a love that will always last.

I hope you learn to love yourself again after a relationship ends. I hope you learn that you are valuable even when alone, even while single.
I hope you find a love that is as strong as the love you've given to those who couldn't love you. I hope you learn to forgive your heart for loving the wrong person.

I hope you find someone who tries for you just as much as you try for them. I hope you find someone who isn't confused about how they feel about you. Someone sure

I hope you find someone who adores your heart, mind and soul.

More than anything, I hope you find someone who reminds you of what love should feel like and what love should be. Someone devoted to helping you maintain your peace

there were those nights
where sadness felt like cold air
and the moon kept the night
from being too dark

you were alone
lying beneath it all
struggling to make sense
of everything that happened

but you kept it altogether
even when you felt like falling apart
you kept hoping for strength
wishing upon dead stars

and you were granted
what you needed

on those nights
lying restless
on a bed of emotional truths

you found more of yourself
and this is when you realized
that you could be everything
you needed and more

444

I hope this reached you…

{Call ends…}

r.h. Sin

Made in the USA
San Bernardino, CA
14 June 2018